# Boston University.

1872–73.

# GENERAL CATALOGUE

OF

# BOSTON UNIVERSITY.

1872-73.

Riverside Press.
1873.

# *ANNOUNCEMENTS.*

*BOSTON UNIVERSITY was incorporated by the General Court of Massachusetts in the year* 1869. *The purpose of its corporators was not the establishment of a College in the ordinary sense of that term, but the building up of a group of collegiate and post-collegiate schools, in which, in the process of time, all forms of higher professional and general education might be conferred. The Charter and General Statutes of the institution contemplate the ultimate organization of at least a dozen distinct colleges and professional schools with as many distinct faculties. Of these three are already in successful operation, to wit, a School of Theology, a School of Law, and a College of Music. Arrangements are in progress for the opening of a School of Medicine and a College of the Liberal Arts the coming autumn.*

## *THE SCHOOL OF THEOLOGY*

*of Boston University, formerly the "Boston Theological Seminary," is now in its twenty-sixth year. It is the largest school of its kind in New England. For special Catalogue and Circular address the Dean, Rev. William F. Warren, D. D.,* 36 *Bromfield Street.*

## *THE SCHOOL OF LAW*

*was opened last fall. It is therefore in its first year. Sixty-five students are in attendance. For terms of admission and other information, address Francis A. Perry, Esq.,* 81 *Washington Street.*

## *THE SCHOOL OF MEDICINE.*

*Time of opening and conditions of admission to be announced by special circular.*

## *THE COLLEGE OF LIBERAL ARTS.*

*This chief Undergraduate College, providing the usual course for the degree of Bachelor of Arts, will be opened next September. Circulars will be ready soon.*

## *THE COLLEGE OF MUSIC,*

*designed exclusively for the graduates of Musical Conservatories and Seminaries, is the first institution of its kind in America. Its facilities for the highest musical culture are believed to be unequaled. Circulars can be obtained by application to the Dean, Dr. E. Tourjée, Music Hall, Boston.*

BOSTON, *March*, 1873.

# CORPORATION.

PRESIDENT.

Ex-Gov. WILLIAM CLAFLIN, LL. D.

VICE PRESIDENT.

Hon. GEORGE F. GAVITT.

SECRETARY.

FRANCIS A. PERRY, Esq.

TREASURER.

A. I. BENYON, Esq.

LEONARD WHITNEY, Esq.
Hon. GEORGE F. GAVITT.
EDWIN H. JOHNSON, Esq.
WILLIAM R. CLARK, D. D.
Hon. JACOB SLEEPER.
Hon. WILLIAM CLAFLIN, LL. D.
Hon. LUCIUS W. POND.
WILLIAM F. WARREN, D. D.
DAVID PATTEN, D. D.
Hon. HENRY O. HOUGHTON.
Bp. GILBERT HAVEN, D. D.
JOEL B. THOMAS, Esq.
JOHN W. LINDSAY, D. D.
JOHN H. TWOMBLY, D. D.
FRANCIS A. PERRY, Esq.
WILLIAM G. LINCOLN, Esq.
Maj. JOSEPH H. CHADWICK.
PLINY NICKERSON, Esq.
HARVEY ARNOLD, Esq.
ABNER I. BENYON, Esq.
DANIEL STEELE, D. D.

# COMMITTEES.

EXECUTIVE COMMITTEE.

| | |
|---|---|
| JACOB SLEEPER, | WILLIAM CLAFLIN, |
| WILLIAM F. WARREN, | WILLIAM R. CLARK. |

FINANCE COMMITTEE.

| | |
|---|---|
| EDWIN H. JOHNSON, | PLINY NICKERSON, |
| DAVID PATTEN, | ABNER I. BENYON. |

STANDING COMMITTEE ON SCHOOL OF THEOLOGY.

WILLIAM F. WARREN, *ex officio*,

| | |
|---|---|
| JACOB SLEEPER, | WILLIAM R. CLARK, |
| DAVID PATTEN, | PLINY NICKERSON. |

STANDING COMMITTEE ON SCHOOL OF LAW.

GEORGE S. HILLARD, *ex officio*,

| | |
|---|---|
| GEORGE F. GAVITT, | FRANCIS A. PERRY, |
| HENRY O. HOUGHTON, | JOHN W. LINDSAY. |

COMMITTEE ON SCHOOL OF MEDICINE.

| | |
|---|---|
| WILLIAM CLAFLIN, | DAVID PATTEN, |
| JACOB SLEEPER, | WILLIAM F. WARREN. |

STANDING COMMITTEE ON COLLEGE OF MUSIC.

EBEN TOURJÉE, *ex officio*,

| | |
|---|---|
| JOSEPH H. CHADWICK, | WILLIAM R. CLARK, |
| LEONARD WHITNEY, | DANIEL STEELE. |

COMMITTEE ON COLLEGE OF THE LIBERAL ARTS.

| | |
|---|---|
| WILLIAM F. WARREN, | GEORGE F. GAVITT, |
| HENRY O. HOUGHTON, | JOSEPH H. CHADWICK, |
| JOHN W. LINDSAY, | WILLIAM R. CLARK, |

DANIEL STEELE.

# OFFICERS

OF

# INSTRUCTION AND GOVERNMENT.

HON. GEORGE S. HILLARD, LL. D.,
DEAN OF THE SCHOOL OF LAW.

PROF. EBEN TOURJÉE, DR. MUS.,
DEAN OF THE COLLEGE OF MUSIC.

REV. WILLIAM F. WARREN, D. D.,
DEAN OF THE SCHOOL OF THEOLOGY.

---

PROF. CHARLES N. ALLEN,
*College of Music,* . . . . . . . . . . . . . . . . VIOLIN.

PROF. SANTIAGO CANCIO BELLO,
*School of Theology,* . . . . . . . . . . . . . . SPANISH.

HON. EDMUND H. BENNETT, LL. D.,
*School of Law,* . . . . . . . . . . . . . . CONTRACTS.

MELVILLE M. BIGELOW, M. A.,
*School of Law,* . BILLS AND NOTES, INSURANCE, AND ESTOPPEL.

PROF. DUDLEY BUCK,
*College of Music,* . . . . . . . . . . . . . . . . ORGAN.

REV. BENJAMIN F. COCKER, D. D.,
*School of Theology,* . . . . . . LECTURER ON PANTHEISM.

PROF. CHARLES R. CROSS,
*College of Music,* . . . . . . . . . . . . . ACOUSTICS.

HON. DWIGHT FOSTER,
*School of Law,* . . . . . . . . . . . . . . . . EQUITY.

PROF. WULF FRIES,
*College of Music,* . . . . . . . . . . . . . VIOLONCELLO.

N. ST. JOHN GREEN, LL. B.,
*School of Law,* . . . . . TORTS AND CRIMES, AND KENT'S COMMENTARIES.

HON. GEORGE S. HILLARD, LL. D.,
*School of Law,* . . . CONTRACTS AND PROFESSIONAL ETHICS.

PROF. CHARLES KOPPITZ,
*College of Music,* . . . . . . . . . . . . ORCHESTRATION.

REV. JACOB F. KRAUSS,
*School of Theology,* . . . . . . . ORIENTAL LANGUAGES.

REV. JAMES E. LATIMER, D. D.,
*School of Theology,* . . . . . . . . HISTORICAL THEOLOGY.

REV. ERNEST H. LESEMAN, M. A.,
*School of Theology,* . . . . . . . . . . . . . . GERMAN.

PROF. THOMAS F. LEONARD,
*School of Theology,* . . . . . . . . . . . . . ELOCUTION.

REV. JOHN W. LINDSAY, D. D.,
*School of Theology,* . . . . . . . EXEGETICAL THEOLOGY.

HON. FRANCIS J. LIPPITT,
*School of Law,* . . . . . . . . PARTNERSHIP AND AGENCY.

HON. OTIS P. LORD,
*School of Law,* . . . . . . . . PLEADINGS AND PRACTICE.

PROF. ALBERT C. MAGGI,
*College of Music,* . . . . . . . . . . . . . . . ITALIAN.

PROF. JOHN O'NEILL,
*College of Music,* ENGLISH AND ITALIAN SINGING, ÆSTHETICS AND PHYSIOLOGY OF THE VOICE.

PROF. JOHN ORDRONAUX, LL. D.,
*School of Law,* . . . . . . . . . MEDICAL JURISPRUDENCE.

HON. HENRY W. PAINE, LL. D.,
*School of Law,* . . . . . . . . . . . . . REAL PROPERTY.

PROF. JOHN KNOWLES PAINE, M. A.,
*College of Music,* . . COMPOSITION, MUSICAL HISTORY AND ÆSTHETICS.

PROF. JAMES C. D. PARKER,
*College of Music,* . . . . . . . . . . . . . PIANO-FORTE.

REV. DAVID PATTEN, D. D.,
*School of Theology,* . . PROFESSOR EMERITUS OF PRACTICAL THEOLOGY, AND LIBRARIAN.

HON. EDWARD L. PIERCE,
*School of Law,* . . . . . . BAILMENTS AND CORPORATIONS.

HON. ROBERT C. PITMAN, LL. D.,
*School of Law,* . . . . . . . . . . . . . MOOT COURTS.

REV. JOHN MORRISON REID, D. D.,
*School of Theology,* . . . . . . . . LECTURER ON MISSIONS.

HON. CHARLES T. RUSSELL,
*School of Law,* . . . . . . . . EVIDENCE AND ADMIRALTY.

HON. BENJAMIN F. THOMAS,
*School of Law,* . . . . . . . WILLS AND ADMINISTRATIONS.

PROF. EBEN TOURJÉE, DR. MUS.,
*College of Music,* . . . THEORY AND PRACTICE OF SACRED MUSIC.

REV. LUTHER T. TOWNSEND, D. D.,
*School of Theology,* . . . . . . . . PRACTICAL THEOLOGY.

REV. STEPHEN H. TYNG, D, D.,
*School of Theology,* . . . LECTURER ON PASTORAL TOPICS.

REV. WILLIAM F. WARREN, D. D.,
*School of Theology,* . . . . . . . . SYSTEMATIC THEOLOGY.

PROF. FRANCIS WHARTON, LL. D.,
*School of Law,* . . . . . . . . . . . CONFLICT OF LAWS.

BISHOP ISAAC W. WILEY, D. D.,
*School of Theology,* . . . . LECTURER ON THE CHRISTIAN MINISTRY.

REV. THEODORE D. WOOLSEY, D. D., LL. D.,
*School of Theology,* . . . . . . LECTURER ON POLYTHEISM.

PROF. CARL ZERRAHN,
*College of Music,* . . ORATORIO AND ORCHESTRAL CONDUCTOR.

# STUDENTS.

| NAMES. | RESIDENCES. | SCHOOL OR COLLEGE. |
|---|---|---|
| Charles H. Adams, | *Haverhill, Mass.,* | Law. |
| Charles J. Adams, A. B. (*Mt. Union College*), | *Brownsville, Pa.,* | Theology. |
| Walter Adams, A. B. (*Harvard College*), | *Framingham, Mass.,* | Law. |
| J. Henry Allen, A. B. (*Dartmouth College*), | *Surry, N. H.,* | Theology. |
| William P. Austin, A. B. (*Harvard College*), | *Boston, Mass.,* | Law. |
| Benjamin Franklin Armstrong, A. B. (*Dickinson College*), | *London, O.,* | Law. |
| Charles Clarence Barton, A. B. (*Trinity College*), | *Belmont, Mass.,* | Law. |
| Francis Bassett, A. B. (*Harvard College*), | *Boston, Mass.,* | Law. |
| Clark Asa Batchelder, | *Manchester, Vt.,* | Law. |
| John H. Bates, | *Hermitage, Pa.,* | Theology. |
| Samuel L. Beiler, A. B. (*Ohio Wesleyan University*), | *Lima, O.,* | Theology. |
| William E. Bennett, | *Goffstown, N. H.,* | Theology. |
| George W. Bent, | *Antwerp, N. Y.,* | Theology. |
| Leonard Byrne Blake, A. B. (*Kenyon College*), | *Gambier, O.,* | Law. |
| Jarvis Blume, | *Boston, Mass.,* | Law. |
| Otis Lafayette Bonney, | *Hanson, Mass.,* | Law. |
| James Iverson Boswell, A. B. (*University of Pennsylvania*), | *Philadelphia, Pa.,* | Theology. |
| Everett A. Boyden, | *Perry, Me.,* | Theology. |
| James Higginson Bowditch, A. B. (*Harvard College*), | *Brookline, Mass.,* | Law. |
| Benjamin Francis Briggs, Attorney, | *Stoneham, Mass.,* | Law. |
| Marcus D. Buell, A. B. (*University of New York*), | *Williamsburg, N. Y.,* | Theology. |
| A. W. Bunker, | *Haverhill, Mass.,* | Theology |
| Charles Joseph Burns, | *Chelsea, Mass.,* | Law. |

| | | |
|---|---|---|
| Joseph Edward Buswell, | *Lawrence, Mass.,* | Law. |
| George H. Butler, | *E. Greenwich, R. I.,* | Theology. |
| John W. Butler, | *Passaic, N. J.,* | Theology. |
| George W. Buzzell, | *East Benton, Me.,* | Theology. |
| | | |
| David D. Cheney, A. B. (*Ohio Wesleyan University*), | *Xenia, O.,* | Theology. |
| Frank Linus Child, A. B. (*Brown University*), | *Worcester, Mass.,* | Law. |
| Davis W. Clark, A. B. (*Ohio Wesleyan University*), | *Cincinnati, O.,* | Theology. |
| Henry H. Clark, | *Calais, Me.,* | Theology. |
| Thomas Clithero, A. B. (*Lawrence University*), | *Portage City, Wis.,* | Theology. |
| Cyrus Cobb, | *Cambridgeport, Mass.,* | Law. |
| David S. Coles, A. B. (*College of New Jersey*), | *Elizabeth, N. J.,* | Theology. |
| Richard W. Copeland, A. B. (*Syracuse University*), | *Clarendon, N. Y.,* | Theology. |
| Samuel P. Craver, A. B. (*Iowa College*), | *Grinnell, Iowa,* | Theology. |
| Charles A. Cressy, | *Hudson, N. H.,* | Theology. |
| James R. Crofoot, | *Constableville, N. Y.,* | Theology. |
| Samuel S. Curry, A. B. (*E. Tennessee Wesleyan University*), | *Athens, Tenn.,* | Theology. |
| John R. Cushing, A. B. (*Wesleyan University*), | *Auburndale, Mass.,* | Theology. |
| | | |
| J. Alphonso Day, A. B. (*Wesleyan University*), | *Winthrop, Mass.,* | Theology. |
| Josiah W. Dearborn, A. B. (*Dartmouth College*), | *Salem Depot, N. H.,* | Theology. |
| Charles G. Deming, A. M. (*Baker University*), | *Leavenworth, Kan.,* | Theology. |
| Alexander Dight, A. B. (*Alleghany College*), | *Mercer, Pa.,* | Theology. |
| Charles W. Drees, A. B. (*Ohio Wesleyan University*), | *Xenia, O.,* | Theology. |
| Charles Acton Drew, A. B. (*Harvard College*), | *Chelsea, Mass.,* | Law. |
| George W. Dubois, A. B. (*Ohio Wesleyan University*), | *Cincinnati, O.,* | Theology. |
| Charles H. Dunton, A. B. (*University of Vermont*), | *Underhill, Vt.,* | Theology. |
| Jesse M. Durrell, | *East Boston, Mass.,* | Theology. |
| William E. Dwight, A. B. (*Wesleyan University*), | *Chelsea, Mass.,* | Theology. |

|  |  |  |
|---|---|---|
| John H. Emerson, A. B. (*Wesleyan University*), | *Watertown, Mass.*, | Theology. |
| Ephraim Emerton, A. B. (*Harvard College*), | *Salem, Mass.*, | Law. |
| Andrew Otis Evans, A. B. (*Harvard College*), | *Boston, Mass.*, | Law. |
| Schuyler C. Farnham, A. B. (*Dartmouth College*), | *Topsham, N. H.*, | Theology. |
| Robert W. C. Farnsworth, A. B. (*Wesleyan University*), | *Ft. Edward, N. Y.*, | Theology. |
| Henry Parker Fellows, A. B., Att'y (*Yale College*), | *Boston, Mass.*, | Law. |
| Edwin C. Ferguson, A. M. (*University of Vermont*), | *Burlington, Vt.*, | Theology. |
| Sarah C. Fisher, | *Cambridgeport, Mass.*, | Music. |
| Willis Everett Flint, | *Danvers, Mass.*, | Law. |
| George Sumner Forbush, | *Boston, Mass.*, | Law. |
| George Whitefield Foster, Attorney, | *Andover, Mass.*, | Law. |
| William W. Foster, Jr., | *East Dorset, Vt.*, | Theology. |
| Daniel Frawley, | *Brookline, Mass.*, | Law. |
| James W. Fulton, | *Manchester, N. H.*, | Theology. |
| John W. Gaddis, A. B. (*Ohio Wesleyan University*), | *Ripley, O.*, | Theology. |
| Owen Augustus Galvin, | *Boston, Mass.*, | Law. |
| Elijah George, | *New Rochelle, N. Y.*, | Law. |
| Franklin D. Goodrich, | *Bow, N. H.*, | Theology. |
| Arling F. Goodyear, | *Boston, Mass.*, | Music. |
| Charles P. Gorely, A. B., Attorney (*Harvard College*), | *Boston, Mass.*, | Law. |
| Thomas W. Gregory. | *Burlington, Vt.*, | Theology. |
| Peter Stinger Grosscup, A. B. (*Wittenberg College*), | *Ashland, O.*, | Law. |
| Almon E. Hall, A. B. (*Wesleyan University*), | *Stamford, Vt.*, | Theology. |
| Joseph B. B. Hamilton, A. B. (*Mt. Union College*), | *Somerville, Mass.*, | Theology. |
| L. L. H. Hamilton, A. B. (*Mt. Union College*), | *Mt. Union, O.*, | Theology. |
| William Henry Hart, | *Chelsea, Mass.*, | Law. |
| Henry Francis Harris, A. B. (*Tufts College*), | *Oakdale, Mass.*, | Law. |
| William H. Haskell, A. M. (*Alleghany College*), | *Perry, O.*, | Theology. |
| David Greene Haskins, Attorney, | *Cambridge, Mass.*, | Law. |

| | | |
|---|---|---|
| George Warren Hayford, | *Boston, Mass.,* | Law. |
| Eugene C. Herdman, | *Westford, N. Y.,* | Theology. |
| Alphonso E. Higgens, | *Feesburg, O.,* | Theology. |
| George Trask Higley, A. B. (*Amherst College*), | *Ashland, Mass.,* | Law. |
| Franklin A. Hill, | *Hudson, N. H.,* | Theology. |
| Joseph A. Hines, | *Boston, Mass.,* | Law. |
| Elias Hodge, | *Fort Scott, Kan.,* | Theology. |
| Raymond E. Holway, A. B. (*Harvard College*), | *Chelsea, Mass.,* | Theology. |
| Wesley O. Holway, A. M. (*Harvard College*), | *Charlestown, Mass.,* | Theology. |
| Francis D. Hornbrook, A. B. (*Ohio University*), | *Wheeling, W. Va.,* | Theology. |
| William Henshaw Horton, Jr., | *Watertown, Mass.,* | Law. |
| Henry Clarence Hubbard, | *Boston, Mass.,* | Law. |
| James H. Humphrey, A. B. (*Lawrence University*), | *Sheboygan Falls, Wis.,* | Theology. |
| Edward Mills Hunt, | *Weymouth, Mass.,* | Law. |
| William E. Huntington, A. B. (*University of Wisconsin*), | *Marshall, Wis.,* | Theology. |
| Edward L. Hyde, | *Hanover, Mass.,* | Theology. |
| George S. Innis, A. B. (*Ohio Wesleyan University*), | *Columbus, O.,* | Theology. |
| Frank P. Ireland, | *Newburyport, Mass.,* | Law. |
| Byron Berkley Johnson, | *Waltham, Mass.,* | Law. |
| John Jarman, | *Llanidloes, Wales,* | Theology. |
| Richard F. Kay, | *Chicago, Ill.,* | Theology. |
| Albert J. Kirkland, | *New Bedford, Mass.,* | Theology. |
| Matthias M. Kugler, A. B. (*Ohio Wesleyan University*), | *Goshen, O.,* | Theology. |
| Ernest H. Leseman, A. B. (*Ohio Wesleyan University*), | *Nashville, Ill.,* | Theology. |
| Selwyn Lynde, | *Melrose, Mass.,* | Law. |
| John Oliver McClintock, A. B. (*Alleghany College*), | *Meadville, Pa.,* | Law. |
| John T. McFarland, A. B. (*Simpson Centenary College*), | *Mt. Pleasant, Iowa,* | Theology. |
| James A. McGeough, A. B. (*Boston College*), | *Boston, Mass.,* | Law. |
| Wilbur F. Mappin, | *Greensburg, Ind.,* | Theology. |
| Joel Martin, | *New Salem, N Y.,* | Theology. |

| | | |
|---|---|---|
| Virgil W. Mattoon, A. B. (*Wesleyan University*), | *Cazenovia, N. Y.*, | Theology. |
| William H. Meredith, | *Gorham, N. H.*, | Theology. |
| Frederick M. Miller, | *Northfield, N. H.*, | Theology. |
| Frank Morrell, | *Boston Mass.*, | Law. |
| James W. Morris, A. B. (*Lincoln University*), | *Providence, R. I.*, | Theology. |
| Walter Scott Morrison, A. B. (*Dickinson College*), | *Bendersville, Pa.*, | Theology. |
| Charles R. Morse, | *Natick, Mass.*, | Law. |
| Charles W. Mossell, A. B. (*Lincoln University*), | *Lockport, N. Y.*, | Theology. |
| William Bernard Murphy, A. B. (*Santa Clara College*), | *San Jose, Cal.*, | Law. |
| William Albion Nason, | *Kennebunk, Me.*, | Law. |
| Gilbert C. Osgood, | *Marblehead, Mass.*, | Theology. |
| John P. Otis, A. M. (*University of New York*), | *Brooklyn, N. Y.*, | Theology. |
| Isabella G. Parker, | *Auburndale, Mass.*, | Music. |
| William J. Parkinson, | *South Lawrence, Mass.*, | Theology. |
| William M. Patterson, A. B. (*Ohio Wesleyan University*), | *Cincinnati, O.*, | Theology. |
| William M. Perkins, | *Cambridge, Mass.*, | Music. |
| Willard F. Perrin, A. B. (*Harvard College*), | *Grantville, Mass.*, | Theology. |
| William H. Peters, A. B. (*Wesleyan University*), | *Green Haven, N. Y.*, | Theology. |
| Charles F. Phillips, | *Hanover, Mass.*, | Law. |
| Watson L. Phillips, A. B. (*Wesleyan University*), | *Salem, N. Y.*, | Theology. |
| John D. Pickles, | *Annapolis, N. S.*, | Theology. |
| John Edward Pike, A. B. (*Dartmouth College*), | *Rollinsford, N. H.*, | Law. |
| Damon C. Porter, A. B. (*Wesleyan University*), | *Boston, Mass.*, | Theology. |
| Louis F. Postle, A. B. (*Ohio Wesleyan University*), | *Columbus, O.*, | Theology. |
| Arnold Augustus Rand, | *Boston, Mass.*, | Law. |
| Bradford Raymond, A. B. (*Lawrence University*), | *Stamford, Conn.*, | Theology. |
| Benjamin Calvin Reed, | *E. Bridgewater, Mass.*, | Law. |
| Louis A. Retts, | *Economy, Ind.*, | Theology. |
| William G. Richardson, | *Lewiston, Me.*, | Theology |

| | | |
|---|---|---|
| William N. Roberts, | *Chelsea, Vt.*, | Theology. |
| Isaac F. Row, | *Plymouth, England*, | Theology. |
| T. Veeraragava Row, *alias*, John Robert Bruce, | *Madras, India*, | Theology. |
| Mark R. Rowse, A. B. (*Queen's College*), | *Bath, Canada*, | Theology. |
| Charles W. Ryder, | *Medford, Mass.*, | Theology. |
| Wilbur Fisk Sandford, A. B. (*Wesleyan University*), | *Long Plain, Mass.*, | Theology. |
| John Henry Sherburne, | *Charlestown, Mass.*, | Law. |
| Samuel W. Siberts, B. S. (*Iowa Wesleyan University*), | *Winfield, Iowa*, | Theology. |
| Henry J. Small, | *York, Pa.*, | Music. |
| Joseph Adams Smith, | *Boston, Mass.*, | Law. |
| Theophilus Gilman Smith, A. B. (*Harvard College*), | *Somerville, Mass.*, | Law. |
| Silas Sprowls, A. B. (*Alleghany College*), | *Clayville, Pa.*, | Theology. |
| Wilbur Fisk Steele, A. B. (*Syracuse University*), | *Boston, Mass.*, | Theology. |
| John A. Story, A. B. (*Ohio Wesleyan University*), | *Bowersville, O.*, | Theology. |
| Theodore Sutro, A. B. (*Harvard College*), | *New York City*, | Law. |
| Charles W. Taylor, | *Laconia, N. H.*, | Theology. |
| Charles S. Thornton, A. B. (*Harvard College*), | *Boston, Mass.*, | Law. |
| Alfred Turner, | *St. Albans, Me.*, | Music. |
| John S. Van Cleve, A. B. (*Ohio Wesleyan University*), | *Cincinnati, O.*, | Theology. |
| William H. Vandervoort, | *Boston, Mass.*, | Law. |
| Edwin P. Walker, Attorney, | *Charlestown, Mass.*, | Law. |
| Henry A. Walker, Attorney, | *Charlestown, Mass.*, | Law. |
| George B. Waters, | *Worcester, Mass.*, | Law. |
| David Kemper Watson, A. B. (*Dickinson College*), | *London, O.*, | Law. |
| James J. Watts, A. B. (*Central College*), | *Fayette, Mo.*, | Theology. |
| Francis Clarke Welch, Attorney, | *Waltham, Mass.*, | Law. |
| F. M. Wheeler, | *Moradabad, India*, | Theology. |
| William F. Whitcher, A. B. (*Wesleyan University*), | *Woodsville, N. H.*, | Theology. |
| Samuel B. Whitney, | *Cambridge, Mass.*, | Music. |

| Name | Residence | School |
|---|---|---|
| Carlton C. Wilbor, A. B. (*Syracuse University*), | *Maplewood, Mass.*, | Theology. |
| Charles Amory Williams, A. B. (*Harvard College*), | *Boston, Mass.*, | Law. |
| Charles Garrison Wilson, | *Chelsea, Mass.*, | Law. |
| Cortlandt Wood, A. B. (*Yale College*), | *Webster, Mass.*, | Law. |
| Joseph R. Wood, A. B. (*Wesleyan University*), | *Michigan City, Ind.*, | Theology. |
| Frank Galloupe Woodbury, | *Lynn, Mass.*, | Law. |
| George Franklin Woodward, A. B. (*Williams College*), | *Lowell, Mass.*, | Law. |
| George W. Wright, A. B. (*Wesleyan University*), | *Beekman, N. Y.*, | Theology. |
| Walter J. Yates, | *Providence, R. I.*, | Theology. |
| Edmund Rex Zimmerman, A. M. (*Marshall College*), | *Schaeferstown, Pa.*, | Theology. |
| Jonathan Zook, A. B. (*Ohio Wesleyan University*), | *Wooster, O.*, | Theology. |

## SUMMARY.

| | |
|---|---|
| Students in School of Theology . . . . . . | 105 |
| Students in School of Law . . . . . . . | 65 |
| Students in College of Music . . . . . . . | 7 |
| Total . . . . . . . | 177 |

UNIVERSITAS BOSTONIENSIS.
CONDITA MDCCCLXIX.

www.ingramcontent.com/pod-product-compliance
Lightning Source LLC
LaVergne TN
LVHW020635110826
845149LV00004B/1201
*9781418191252*